Listen Up! Speak Up!

Listen Up! Speak Up!

The Third Book of Speaking Up:
A Plain Text Guide to Advocacy

John Tufail and Kate Lyon

Jessica Kingsley Publishers
London and Philadelphia

First published in New Zealand in 2005
by People's Advocacy Network

This edition first published in 2007
by Jessica Kingsley Publishers
116 Pentonville Road
London N1 9JB, UK
and
400 Market Street, Suite 400
Philadelphia, PA 19106, USA

www.jkp.com

Library of Congress Cataloging in Publication Data
A CIP catalog record for this book is available from the Library of Congress

British Library Cataloguing in Publication Data
A CIP catalogue record for this book is available from the British Library

ISBN 978 1 84310 477 3

Printed and bound in the People's Republic of China
by Nanjing Amity Printing
APC-FT4808-3

'To teach a man how he may learn
to grow independently, and for himself,
is the greatest service
that one man can do another.'
Benjamin Jowett

Contents

1. Be Strong for Yourself and Others

In this part of the **four books of speaking up** we will be talking as if you are the advocate – and you have an advocacy partner! But remember, it will be the same if you are advocating for yourself!

Advocacy is always about speaking up in the right way. Being able to speak up properly so that people will listen to you and actually hear what you are saying isn't easy for anyone. Even prime ministers and presidents find it difficult sometimes. So if you find speaking up difficult, don't worry, it happens to everybody!

Like everything else, the more you practise speaking up, the easier it gets. At the beginning it can be very hard. But there are some things that you can learn that will make it easier for you.

There is jargon for learning to speak up for yourself and being heard. It is called **assertiveness training**. All this means is that people have to learn how to be strong for themselves. It means that everyone has a right to be heard and that everyone must be treated fairly. This is your right!

It also means that you have to respect the rights of other people at the same time.

Some people keep quiet:

- because they want to be nice and not cause trouble

or

- because they feel that the person or people they are talking to might get angry and punish them in some way.

They think that there's no point because other people are stronger than them. So they smile and say thank you, even though they know that they haven't been given what they need – even though they know they have a right to what they are asking for.

Then they think everyone will like them. No-one will get angry with them. But when this happens:

- no-one will listen to them

- no-one will see them

- no-one will respect them.

So when they want something important they will be ignored. Because they will be seen as someone who doesn't really bother how they are treated.

This doesn't mean that people have to be selfish! Or loud! Or rude! In fact it means almost the opposite.

Before you can speak to be heard, you have to learn to listen.

- You have to learn that everyone sees things in different ways.

- You have to learn that the only way to get what you need is to get people to agree with you.

- You have to learn that there is a difference between talking AT people and talking WITH people.

- You have to learn that there is a difference between being silent – listening and learning – and being afraid to speak.

Before we go any further it might be a good idea to read Roy's story.

2. Roy's Story

Nobody would listen to Roy.

Roy lived with his mother and two sisters in a very nice house in the suburbs of a large city.

Roy had lived all his life with a condition called cerebral palsy. This meant that he couldn't use his body very well. He could use one arm and hand enough to write with, but it was hard and took a long time. His hand shook so the writing was like a spider making patterns on the paper. At least that's how Roy described it!

Roy also had some difficulty speaking. He could speak OK, but he had to speak very slowly and his words ran into each other a bit. You had to listen properly to hear his words. It was a bit like a slightly deaf person having to listen to anybody! Because Roy found it difficult to speak, nobody would take the time to listen to him. Not his family. Not his teachers. Not his social worker.

Because Roy had difficulty in getting other people to understand him, people thought he was not very clever. He had been diagnosed as having a really low intelligence when he was young. A special test called an IQ test said he had an IQ of 36. This is very low. It usually means people can't be trusted to make decisions for themselves.

Everyone believed what this test said. Well...nearly everyone.

Another problem was that Roy came from a culture that said that if a family had someone born into the family who had something wrong with them, it was a sign that somebody in the family had done something wrong in a previous life. Roy's mother had been told this by a Holy Man. He said that Roy was the burden that the family had to carry.

This made Roy's mother ashamed of him. She hid him away as much as she could. He lived in one room and didn't share with the rest of the family. He didn't go out with the family. He wasn't allowed out by himself except to go to school and college. His mother and his sisters thought that Roy was a figure of shame so they wouldn't listen to his needs. He was a punishment.

Roy wasn't very happy. He had made friends at college but couldn't go out with them. He wasn't allowed to go on trips. He wasn't allowed to have any money except for lunch.

Roy had a social worker. He tried to explain his unhappiness to this social worker. But the social worker came from the same culture as Roy's family and could understand why the mother was ashamed. He felt Roy should understand his mother's problem. He thought Roy wasn't able to live independently and that Roy's mother would have to look after Roy all his life. He thought Roy should learn to be grateful to his mother.

One day a new teacher at Roy's college noticed he wasn't very happy. The teacher took time to talk to Roy. The teacher listened to Roy. It was the first time anyone had ever listened to what Roy had to say.

The teacher contacted an advocate. The advocate met Roy at college.

At first Roy found it hard to speak to the advocate. So he took Roy to a café. He told Roy it didn't matter if he didn't want to speak just then, he would be ready for Roy when he wanted to speak.

So a few days later Roy asked the teacher to arrange for the advocate to come and see him. This time Roy felt like speaking. The advocate listened.

Roy said he couldn't go on living at home. He said that with a bit of help he thought he could live by himself, independently.

Roy said he wanted a new social worker who could understand how he felt. He asked the advocate to help him sort things out without his mother or sisters knowing anything. At least until he could move out of the family home. He said his mother would stop him and force him to say he didn't want to move after all.

His mother had all his money. All the benefits he was due were paid to his mother. This had been arranged between a social worker and the mother. They had told him that he had to allow this because his mother was his guardian and he couldn't manage money.

There were a lot of things for Roy and the advocate to think about. They needed a plan! And the most difficult thing was to get things done without his mother finding out.

They wrote a list of the people they would need to speak to. The first thing they decided was that they needed to prove that Roy could live alone if he was given the chance. So they asked some people at the college to write letters about all the things that Roy could do.

The teacher helped a lot. The teacher was able to find out all the things that Roy had been doing:

- He had done a course on cooking and housework. He had done well.

- He had done a course on how to manage money. He had done well.

- He had learned how to write letters and how to store and file things.

- He was learning how to use a computer so that people could understand his writing and so that he could find out things and speak to his friends.

All the teachers who had worked with Roy said they thought he could live by himself if he had some support. They agreed to say this in writing. They said that Roy's biggest problem was that he wasn't allowed to do things at home. They said when they tried to speak to his mother she said she was too busy.

Some of the teachers felt sad that they hadn't taken time to speak to Roy. To listen to Roy.

This was the first bit of the plan.

Then Roy agreed that his advocate should speak to the person who was his social worker's boss! This was scary for Roy because he was afraid his mother would find out. 'I don't trust them,' he said.

The advocate phoned the social worker's manager. He said that he was Roy's advocate and he had a letter from Roy saying this. He said that he could only talk about what Roy wanted if the manager promised to keep everything secret. Especially from Roy's social worker and Roy's family.

The manager said that he couldn't do that because Roy's mother had a right to know everything. Roy's mother was his guardian. Roy's mother also had a piece of paper from a court saying that she could make all his decisions for him, and handle his money. This piece of paper said that Roy's mother held what is called 'an enduring power of attorney'.

The advocate said he had a letter from Roy saying he didn't want his mother to make decisions or look after his money any more. This was called 'revoking' the power of attorney. Roy didn't want anyone making decisions for him any more.

There was also a letter from a psychologist saying that Roy didn't have an IQ of 36 after all. In fact he had a high IQ. Well over one hundred. He just did things differently to most other people. He had worked out his own ways of solving problems.

This was another part of Roy's plan. He wanted to control his own life. He had worked out what to do with his advocate. They had looked it up together on a computer in college.

The advocate said that Roy had a right to privacy. And that meant that everything that happened in the meeting had to be secret – especially from Roy's family.

The manager didn't like it. He said he would have to speak to his bosses. The advocate said that it would be a pity if everything ended up in court. 'Everyone would be hurt,' he said. Finally, the manager said he would accept that Roy had a right to privacy.

Roy and his advocate met with the manager. They met at Roy's college. At the meeting there was a teacher from the college who said that everything about Roy's ability to live alone was true...so long as Roy had some support.

Roy had asked the advocate to tell the manager about everything that was happening to him at home:

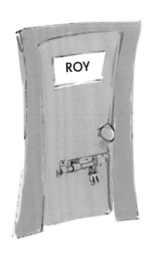

- not being allowed any of his own money

- not being allowed to go out

- not being allowed to go on college trips

- being locked away in his room when friends and family visited, etc., etc.

He wanted the advocate to speak up for him because he wanted to learn how to speak up for himself. He wanted to learn by watching the advocate. So he did.

Roy had asked his advocate to explain about the social worker. So he did.

'Hmmm,' said the manager. 'I think we can say this is abuse... I think you should have a new social worker.'

And Roy was given a new social worker.

Everyone agreed that there should be a big meeting where a plan could be made to help Roy. At the meeting everyone said that it would be a good idea if Roy could move out of his home.

'But we can't do this straight away,' the manager said. 'It all takes time. It might take months... You'll have to be patient, Roy.'

Roy said he wanted to leave the meeting to discuss something with his advocate. He told his advocate that he wasn't going home.

'I'm leaving home NOW,' he said.

'That's your decision,' said the advocate. 'No-one can make you. I'll support whatever you want to do.'

'Thank you,' said Roy. 'That's given me the strength to make my decision... I have a plan!'

'I have a plan!' 'Good for you!' ???????????

'Good for you,' said the advocate. '...Er...what is it?'

'Wait and see,' said Roy.

Roy went back into the meeting and sat and listened while everyone made plans about his future. After everyone (except Roy) had decided what was best for Roy, the manager said, 'Well that's it, it's all decided. Time for you to go home now, Roy.'

'I'm not going anywhere,' said Roy.

'In that case, neither am I,' said the advocate.

'I'm not leaving here until you have found me somewhere to live,' said Roy.

And he stayed.

The manager and everyone else said, 'You can't do this!'

But he did.

And he stayed...until the manager gave in. The manager got on the phone and made a lot of calls and in the end said, 'I've found you somewhere to stay, Roy.'

Roy had learned to speak up.

People had learned to listen to Roy. People had realised that Roy had needs. People had realised that Roy had rights. People had realised that Roy was not stupid, that in fact he was very bright.

Now Roy has the support he needs to live independently. He is at a college learning to be a scientist.

Think about Roy's story as you read the rest of this book.

3. Listening

The first thing you have to learn about speaking up as an advocate is about listening.

People can speak as loud and as long as they want, but if no-one is listening they are wasting their breath. Most of us have found this out the hard way! Meeting an advocate should give people a chance to speak to and with someone who listens.

The problem is that listening, at least listening properly in a way that helps a person speak up, is not as easy as it sounds.

A lot of people act as though they are listening. They might even think they are listening. But they don't really hear, or they only hear what they want to hear.

As an advocate you can't do anything unless you are quite sure of what it is that your partner really needs. And the reason you are with your partner in the first place is because nobody has been listening to him or her – maybe for years!

So why do you think your partner can trust you enough to listen properly? Why do you think your partner is going to trust you enough to tell you about what their needs are? Why should they? Your partner doesn't know you. Never met you before.

You have to earn respect and trust before you can expect someone to tell you anything that is really important to them.

The first step in earning trust and respect is that you have to respect them!

Remember. You are there for your partner, so there are quite a lot of things you have to know about listening. There are some things you must do. There are some things you must NOT do! And there are some traps to avoid.

The first thing to do might happen before you even meet your partner.

You must set a date and time and place to meet that will make your partner feel comfortable.

This can be difficult, because often you will find that the meeting is arranged with someone else. It might be a carer, like a parent, or a support worker or a teacher. And when this happens you can never be sure whether the date and time and place is best for your partner – or best for the person who has arranged the meeting.

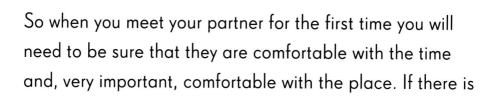

So when you meet your partner for the first time you will need to be sure that they are comfortable with the time and, very important, comfortable with the place. If there is someone else who wants to be at the meeting you have to be sure the partner is comfortable with that. That the partner agrees – even if it is a parent or other family member.

You see, it is easy to think that if the meeting is in the partner's own home, then that will be OK. That is, you assume that they are comfortable there. But what if the problem is actually about their home? Or someone living or working there is the problem? Then you might find that somewhere away from home would be best. You need to find out.

home sweet home

So the first meeting might just be to find out where and when your partner wants to meet for a proper conversation.

But don't think this is a waste of time. It will help your partner realise that they are in control. This may never have happened before! So even arranging the first meeting is important in getting the trust of your partner.

But some other things might happen before you first meet your partner. Things that might affect the way you think about your partner. For example, someone might 'warn' you about your partner, saying something like: 'Oh, he doesn't understand anything' or 'She is really naughty, always shouting and won't do as she is told' or 'He can't be trusted with money'.

There is nothing wrong with listening to this. Politely and patiently. It's useful to know what other people think.

But when you are with your partner you have to put all this out of your mind. If you don't, you won't be listening to what your partner is telling you. Instead you'll be listening to what other people have told you. You won't be giving your partner a chance to be heard. You won't be giving yourself a chance to listen.

And don't forget, when you learn to work like this with your partner, you will also be learning that this is a good way to treat everyone.

So listening is important. But so is how people see you.

Before you can have a chance to speak up in a way that people will listen and respect what you say, they will judge you by how you look and what you do.

When you first meet your advocacy partner, remember that first appearances are important.

- Be clean and smart – it's a sign of respect.

- Be on time – it's a sign of respect and shows you are acting professionally.

- Be pleasant and polite.

Remember, where you are seated is important in letting the partner know you respect him or her. Don't sit in a place that might make him feel scared or nervous. Too close, for example, or behind a big desk with the partner looking up at you!

Make sure the partner is comfortable.

- Sit where the partner can see and hear you clearly.

- Introduce yourself clearly.

- Don't start the conversation by saying you only have half an hour because you have another appointment!

- Make your partner feel that you are there just for them, for as long as it takes.

Believe that this is true! And let yourself be guided by the partner. Let them ask the questions as much as possible. Give them plenty of time to get their ideas together.

Remember, advocacy partners might be nervous. Might be a bit confused. They might have a lot to say but don't know how to say it. Often the way they want to say things will be their own special way (like Roy). You have to learn from your partners.

Be patient – there's nothing wrong with a bit of silence so long as the partner seems comfortable.

It might take some time before a partner feels like talking about what the problem is. Or sometimes they will just come straight out with it.

Whatever they do, just remember this is the partner's time to speak. You only speak to help the partner get their thoughts together and explain things. You might have to help, but don't ask leading questions.

For example, 'The food here is awful, isn't it?' is a leading question, but 'What's the food like here?' is not.

A good way to find out the problem is sometimes to ask what it is the person likes.

People feel more comfortable talking about what they like. It sometimes makes them think of what it is they don't like and they will talk about these things then.

But you are there to listen.

If you want to write things down you must ask permission of the partner. Writing things down is usually good – but not if it makes the partner uncomfortable. If there's a problem, write things down later.

If you write things down at any time, you must always check that what you have written down is what the partner meant to say. Language can be confusing sometimes, and people can get the wrong impression. So check. Make sure you understand exactly what the partner is really saying.

You might want to use a tape recorder. Again, ask permission.

Body language is important in listening. You have to listen with your whole body. It is important that the way you sit helps explain that you are interested in what the partner is saying.

Don't do things like:

- look out the window

- look at your watch every five minutes

- watch what other people are doing.

You have to concentrate on why you are there. If you start thinking of other things when the partner is speaking, it will show and you will lose the partner's respect.

4. Points of View

Everyone is different. Everyone sees things in a slightly different way.

People have different ways of living, different religions, different experiences, different likes and dislikes. This means that everyone has a different point of view.

An important part of speaking up is learning to recognise these differences and respecting them. If you don't respect other people's differences and point of view, then they won't respect yours. They won't want to listen to you because you will have shown them that you don't want to listen to them.

So even if you disagree completely with someone's point of view, you have to try very hard to find things to agree with. When you find something you both agree with, it becomes easier to talk about other things.

Your point of view!

Remember that speaking up is making sure that people hear your point of view about something important. It might be something important about you, or something important about someone else. Someone you are advocating with.

So far, we have been talking about respecting people and getting respect in return. But once you have that respect, you have to use it to let people understand what your needs are. This means that when you talk to someone you have to be sure in your own mind what it is you want. You need to be clear that the words you use – and the way that you use them – will help you get what you want.

You should also have in your mind not only everything that you would really like to have, but also what is the least that you are prepared to accept.

Remember...

there is a big difference between what you NEED and what you WANT.

Here is an example.

David's story

David, who can't get around without a wheelchair, needs someone with him whenever he goes out. At the moment he only receives care support for four hours at weekends. He thinks this is not right.

He wants to go out more. He likes watching sport. He likes going to the cinema. He can't do this unless there is someone to go with him. David wants 20 hours of support at weekends.

This is what he tells his social worker. The social worker says this is impossible because there is not enough money to pay for the care. David insists that he has a right to live a full life and that to do this he needs 20 hours.

After a long discussion, where David remains firm that he has a right to a full life, the social worker agrees that David should have 16 hours of care.

David is pleased with this because he can still do all the things he wants with 16 hours of care. This is the minimum that he wanted. In fact, this is what he NEEDS to live a full life.

The social worker is pleased because she sees that she has saved some money that can be spent on somebody else.

David was able to see the social worker's point of view, so he was prepared to accept a little bit less. By doing this, he ended up getting what he actually needed to live a full life.

If we look a bit closer at what happened between David and the social worker we can see that being strong for himself involved a number of things:

- He had a clear idea of what he wanted and what was the least he would accept.

- He had a clear idea of his needs – he was able to say exactly what he needed and why.

- He was able to say that he had a right to what he asked for. This meant that the social worker understood him clearly.

- He understood the social worker's point of view, so he was able to ask for what he wanted in a way that did not make the social worker angry or defensive.

Now imagine if David had behaved differently. What do you think would have happened if he had got angry with the social worker when she first said that he couldn't have what he wanted?

What do you think would have happened if he had said, 'I want this and I won't listen to anything else!'?

Do you think that he would have got anything out of the meeting?

5. Speaking Up in Meetings

If you can learn all the things we've just talked about, you will find speaking up becomes much easier – especially when you are only speaking to one person.

However, quite a lot of the time you will have to speak up for what you need in meetings where more than two people are there. You might have to speak up for yourself or for someone else.

The type of meeting that will be most important for you will be meetings about you – or about somebody you are advocating with. So that is what we will talk about.

There are basically two types of meeting that will be about you or your advocacy partner:

There will be the meeting that YOU call to discuss something important to you or your partner.

There will be the meeting that someone else calls to discuss something to do with you or your partner that THEY think is important.

Arranging meetings

If you or your advocate partner want the meeting it means there is something you want. This means that you have to make sure that the people you want at the meeting will come. And you want to make sure that when they come to the meeting, they will be comfortable and will want to listen to what you have to say.

So...

as far as possible you let them have a big say in WHEN the meeting will be and WHERE the meeting will be held.

It is also very important that you tell them exactly what the meeting is going to be about. This is called having an **agenda**. This is important for the following reasons:

- They are more likely to come if you can explain the reason for the meeting clearly.

- They will have time to prepare for the meeting. This will save time and might help you get what you need quicker.

- They are less likely to try and use the meeting for something else (this is called 'setting their own agenda').

- It will help you prepare better for the meeting if you have a clear idea what you want.

Because it is YOUR meeting, you will want to decide exactly what is going to be talked about. So you should write down (or have someone write down for you) what the meeting is going to be about and send it to everyone you have invited. **You set the agenda. You decide who you want to invite.**

Now, if someone else is calling the meeting about something to do with you, it is they that are going to set the agenda.

However, because the meeting is about YOU, you will still have a say about what the meeting is going to be about. After all, you could just say, 'I don't want to talk about this at the moment, thank you.'

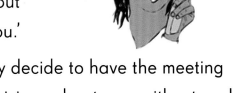

No meeting? Unless they decide to have the meeting without you – and make decisions about you, without you!

Because the meeting is about something to do with you, you can have a big say in when and where the meeting is going to be held. You also have a say about what is going to be talked about. What is on the agenda.

So, whenever possible, if someone is calling a meeting about you it would be a good idea if you could tell them that you would like

to think about the meeting first, before you agree to anything. Doing this means that you can discuss the meeting with someone you trust, and it gives you a chance to think:

- You can think about whether there is anyone you want at the meeting (an advocate for example).

- There might be someone invited to the meeting who you don't want. You might need time to think of the best way of saying you don't want that person there.

- You might need time to work out what is the best time and place for the meeting from your point of view.

- You might want to ask for something else to be discussed at the same time.

When a meeting is about something to do with you, you can and should have a say in nearly everything to do with the meeting – from when and where it is going to be held, to what is going to be talked about and who is going to be there.

Controlling meetings

Now, remember we talked about points of view? Well, even when it is just two people talking together it can be quite difficult to understand each other's point of view. So you can imagine what it will be like when there are three or more people together. Everyone will want their point of view to be heard.

When this happens meetings can get a bit...er...

- **Noisy!** – Everyone trying to speak louder than everyone else so they can be heard.

- **Unfair!** – The loudest, most confident speakers get to take over the meeting, even if what they have to say isn't right or important. Less confident people or people who have difficulty speaking don't get a say.

- **Confusing!** – People start arguing. People start talking about different things. Things get introduced that have nothing to do with the meeting.

Bad meetings are a waste of time!

This is why, even in small meetings, it is important to have:

- An **agenda** (a list of things to be discussed).

> **MEETING**
> 1. Who is at the meeting
> 2. Who is not at the meeting (Apologies)
>
> **AGENDA**
> Things we want to talk about

- **Someone to make a record** of what happened and what decisions are taken.

- A **time limit** (otherwise people will all leave at different times and some things won't be properly heard).

- A **chairperson**.

> MINUTES OF OUR MEETING

The chairperson is in charge of the meeting and is there to make sure that:

- everyone keeps to the point

- everyone is heard properly

- everything on the agenda gets properly discussed

- everyone is polite to each other

- everyone is agreed on any decisions that are taken.

Everyone at the meeting should agree who the chairperson should be before the meeting starts. But at a lot of the sort of meetings you will be involved in, you will find that whoever calls the meeting, or those who see themselves as most important, will try to take charge of the meeting.

This is not a good idea – because the meetings are about YOU or your advocacy partner.

You need to try to control the meeting so that the things YOU think are most important are properly heard and that you have YOUR say. And the best time to do this is at the beginning of the meeting. Then you should find it easier to get everyone to agree that YOU should have a say in who controls the meeting.

It is important to remember that the meeting shouldn't go on if you don't want it to. This means that if you think that:

- things are being said or discussed that you don't like

- someone else is taking over the meeting and this makes you uncomfortable

- you are feeling stressed or tired

- you want to discuss something urgently in private with your advocate,

then you can always stop the meeting for a short time! (Remember, this is what Roy did in the first story.)

If things get too bad, you can always say that you don't want the meeting to continue at all. But you would only do this as a last resort.

Keeping a record

You should always make sure that any decisions taken in a meeting are recorded in a way that is easy to understand. If you don't agree with what is recorded you must say so and get it changed.

MINUTES OF OUR MEETING

Make a record!

It is important that at the end of a meeting you make sure that everything that has been agreed is read out and recorded.

Usually things are recorded in writing. But they don't have to be. There might be a good reason why you would prefer that decisions are recorded in some other way – like on audio tape. Even on video.

If you want to have things recorded in a particular way you must make sure that everything is arranged well before the meeting starts. Otherwise you won't have the right equipment to record things with!

No need to go it alone

Finally, meetings can seem to be quite frightening at times. At other times they can make you angry or frustrated. The worst part of meetings is when people are talking among themselves about you. Sometimes when this happens you feel as though you are not really there. So it does take quite a lot of confidence to feel in control in meetings.

This is why, if you don't feel confident, you should always make sure that you have someone with you who can help build your confidence. It doesn't have to be the person who is

usually your advocate (if you have one). It could be:

- a family member

- a friend

- a member of your faith community

- whoever you can trust and feel comfortable with.

You always have an absolute right to have someone with you at a meeting that is about you!

6. Why Don't You Practise?

You should now have a pretty good idea about the right and wrong ways to speak up.

But reading about speaking up and actually doing it are quite different things! So maybe it would be a good idea if you got together with some friends and practise some of the things we have been talking about.

You could do this in Speaking Up groups – or just among a few people you feel comfortable with. But it would be a good idea if you had someone there who has been through these experiences before.

You could try acting out Roy's story for example. One person could take Roy's role – another could be the advocate and another could be the social work manager maybe? You could have someone else watching and making notes. Then you could all switch roles.

Then you could talk about how it felt. You could talk about any mistakes you think you might have made. You could talk about the good things you think you did.

What is even better is if you can have someone making a video of what you did so you can all watch it together. This can be real fun!

Then you could set up a meeting and try acting out the different roles in a meeting. This is called **role playing**. Role playing is a good and safe way to learn things about yourself. It can help give you confidence.

But it is always a good idea if you can find someone to help you set up the role play if you haven't done it before. This could be anyone who has some experience. It could be a support worker. Or a teacher. But best of all would be someone who has been through the same sort of experiences as you. Why don't you try it?!

And remember. Even just organising some role play is a big part of learning to **speak up for yourself and others**.

GOOD LUCK!